MW00772518

SACRED SPACE

from the website www.sacredspace.ie
Prayer from the Irish Jesuits

LOYOLA PRESS.
A JESUIT MINISTRY

LOYOLA PRESS.
A JESUIT MINISTRY

www.loyolapress.com

This edition of *Sacred Space for Lent* is published by arrangement
with Messenger Publications, 37 Lower Leeson Street, Dublin D02
W938, Ireland.

Scripture quotations are from *New Revised Standard Version Bible:
Anglicised Catholic Edition*, copyright © 1989, 1993 National
Council of the Churches of Christ in the United States of America.
Used by permission. All rights reserved.

Loyola Press in Chicago thanks the Irish Jesuits and Messenger
Press for preparing this book for publication.

Cover art credit: Yifei Fang/Moment/Getty Images

ISBN-13: 978-0-8294-5786-5

Published in Chicago, IL
Printed in the United States of America.
24 25 26 27 28 Versa 10 9 8 7 6 5 4 3 2 1

Contents

Sacred Space Prayer iv

March 5–8 1

First Week of Lent 8

Second Week of Lent 21

Third Week of Lent 38

Fourth Week of Lent 50

Fifth Week of Lent 65

Holy Week 78

Suscipe 107

Prayer to Know God's Will 108

Sacred Space Prayer

Bless all who worship you, almighty God,
from the rising of the sun to its setting;
from your goodness enrich us,
by your love inspire us,
by your Spirit guide us,
by your power protect us,
in your mercy receive us,
now and always.

5–8 March 2025

Something to think and pray about each day this week:

It is no coincidence that Jesus spends forty days in the desert; this is a very particular biblical unit of time. It recalls the Israelites wandering in the desert for forty years before arriving in the Promised Land; the Great Flood lasted forty days; Moses fasted for forty days in the wilderness of Mount Sinai (Deuteronomy 9:18), as did Elijah near Mount Horeb (1 Kings 19:8). We are in good company as we enter into the wilderness, a place where God is revealed. During Lent, it is good for us to remove ourselves from our normal routines, to be still, and to stop and breathe. We need not be afraid of this, for the Gospel shows us that time spent in the wilderness is Spirit-led and we are not alone.

Tríona Doherty and Jane Mellett,
*The Deep End: A Journey with the Sunday Gospels
in the Year of Mark*

The Presence of God

Dear Jesus, today I call on you, but not to ask for anything. I'd like only to dwell in your presence. May my heart respond to your love.

Freedom

God my creator, you gave me life and the gift of freedom. Through your love I exist in this world. May I never take the gift of life for granted. May I always respect others' right to life.

Consciousness

I ask how I am today. Am I particularly tired, stressed or anxious? If any of these characteristics apply, can I try to let go of the concerns that disturb me?

The Word

The word of God comes down to us through the Scriptures. May the Holy Spirit enlighten my mind and my heart to respond to the Gospel teachings. *(Please turn to the Scripture on the following pages. Inspiration points are there, should you need them. When you are ready, return here to continue.)*

Conversation

I begin to talk with Jesus about the Scripture I have just read. What part of it strikes a chord in me? Perhaps the words of a friend—or some story I have heard recently—will rise to the surface in my consciousness. If so, does the story throw light on what the Scripture passage may be saying to me?

Conclusion
Glory be to the Father, and to the Son, and to the Holy Spirit,
As it was in the beginning, is now and ever shall be,
World without end. Amen.

Wednesday 5 March
Ash Wednesday
Matthew 6:1–6, 16–18

'Beware of practising your piety before others in order to be seen by them; for then you have no reward from your Father in heaven.

'So whenever you give alms, do not sound a trumpet before you, as the hypocrites do in the synagogues and in the streets, so that they may be praised by others. Truly I tell you, they have received their reward. But when you give alms, do not let your left hand know what your right hand is doing, so that your alms may be done in secret; and your Father who sees in secret will reward you.

'And whenever you pray, do not be like the hypocrites; for they love to stand and pray in the synagogues and at the street corners, so that they may be seen by others. Truly I tell you, they have received their reward. But whenever you pray, go into your room and shut the door and pray to your Father who is in secret; and your Father who sees in secret will reward you. . . .

'And whenever you fast, do not look dismal, like the hypocrites, for they disfigure their faces so as to show others that they are fasting. Truly I tell you, they have received their reward. But when you fast, put oil on your head and wash your face, so that your fasting may be seen not by others but by your Father who is in secret; and your Father who sees in secret will reward you.'

- Our Father, who sees in secret, looks at our hearts, for it is from there that we truly live. In this season of Lent, which can be a kind of spring-cleaning of our souls, let us begin with generosity in giving more time to prayer and making any sacrifices this might entail, for example, less TV or screen time. We pray to place God more and more at the forefront of our lives.

- When you pray, go into your own heart and shut the door to outward distractions and be with him who is present there. 'Now is the time for prayer, now nothing else matters, now no one is important but God!'

Thursday 6 March
Luke 9:21–25

He sternly ordered and commanded them not to tell anyone, saying, 'The Son of Man must undergo great suffering, and be rejected by the elders, chief priests, and scribes, and be killed, and on the third day be raised.'

Then he said to them all, 'If any want to become my followers, let them deny themselves and take up their cross daily and follow me. For those who want to save their life will lose it, and those who lose their life for my sake will save it. What does it profit them if they gain the whole world, but lose or forfeit themselves?'

- Jesus would have been familiar with the account of the suffering servant in Isaiah 52. Knowing that he was destined to suffer and be killed must have been a heavy burden to carry. We can talk to him about this and ask for some of his courage in facing our own crosses.

- A disciple cannot be above his/her Master. As Christ suffered, so will those who follow him, but the suffering will be different and unique to each one. As writer Alan Jones put it, 'Life is about being dispossessed of everything so that we might possess everything.' We have to lose the false life that is centred on our ego. We pray for insight and the courage to accept our crosses.

Friday 7 March
Matthew 9:14–15

Then the disciples of John came to him, saying, 'Why do we and the Pharisees fast often, but your disciples do not fast?' And Jesus said to them, 'The wedding-guests cannot mourn as long as the bridegroom is with them, can they? The days will come when the bridegroom is taken away from them, and then they will fast.'

- New skins for the new wine of the kingdom of God. There is a time for everything under heaven, a time to be joyful, a time to mourn, a time to fast, and a time to refrain from fasting. Fasting can be helpful to our bodies and can train us to be more disciplined in how we live our Christian lives. As we read in the Book of Wisdom, 'The beginning of wisdom is the most sincere desire for instruction.' We pray for the grace to make a decision for God and for the courage to be faithful to it.

Saturday 8 March
Luke 5:27–32

After this he went out and saw a tax-collector named Levi, sitting at the tax booth; and he said to him, 'Follow me.' And he got up, left everything, and followed him.

Then Levi gave a great banquet for him in his house; and there was a large crowd of tax-collectors and others sitting at the table with them. The Pharisees and their scribes were complaining to his disciples, saying, 'Why do you eat and drink with tax-collectors and sinners?' Jesus answered, 'Those who are well have no need of a physician, but those who are sick; I have come to call not the righteous but sinners to repentance.'

- We do not know how often Matthew had listened to Jesus preaching and teaching, but when the call came to him he was ready to respond to it. Let us pray to be open to whatever God calls us to.

- God loves each person with an infinite and unchanging love. Jesus always saw beyond the outward appearance of those he encountered to the deeper yearnings in their hearts. He said, 'I came that they may have life, and have it abundantly.' He loved the sinner but hated the sin. Let us share with him what is deepest in our hearts.

9–15 March 2025

Something to think and pray about each day this week:

There is a Zen proverb, 'Let go or be dragged', and no one wants to be dragged around the place. Lent invites us to embrace this wilderness time. As we fast from things that are not life-giving for us we are also actively making space for God to breathe life and love into our hearts once more. We do this in the trust that God who loves us wants us to choose life and to clear out the blocks that stand in our way. This is 'good news', a true *metanoia* (a change of heart). God's Kingdom is being fulfilled in us and around us, not yet complete, but with every trip into the wilderness we edge closer to that reality. May this Lenten season be a period of grace.

Tríona Doherty and Jane Mellett,
The Deep End: A Journey with the Sunday Gospels
in the Year of Mark

The Presence of God

Dear Lord, as I come to you today, fill my heart, my whole being, with the wonder of your presence. Help me remain receptive to you as I put aside the cares of this world. Fill my mind with your peace.

Freedom

Lord, grant me the grace to be free from the excesses of this life. Let me not get caught up with the desire for wealth. Keep my heart and mind free to love and serve you.

Consciousness

I exist in a web of relationships: links to nature, people, God. I trace out these links, giving thanks for the life that flows through them. Some links are twisted or broken; I may feel regret, anger, disappointment. I pray for the gift of acceptance and forgiveness.

The Word

God speaks to each of us individually. I listen attentively to hear what he is saying to me. Read the text a few times, then listen. *(Please turn to the Scripture on the following pages. Inspiration points are there, should you need them. When you are ready, return here to continue.)*

Conversation

Jesus, you speak to me through the words of the Gospels. May I respond to your call today. Teach me to recognise your hand at work in my daily living.

Conclusion

I thank God for these moments we have spent together and for any insights I have been given concerning the text.

Sunday 9 March
First Sunday of Lent

Luke 4:1–13

Jesus, full of the Holy Spirit, returned from the Jordan and was led by the Spirit in the wilderness, where for forty days he was tempted by the devil. He ate nothing at all during those days, and when they were over, he was famished. The devil said to him, 'If you are the Son of God, command this stone to become a loaf of bread.' Jesus answered him, 'It is written, "One does not live by bread alone."'

Then the devil led him up and showed him in an instant all the kingdoms of the world. And the devil said to him, 'To you I will give their glory and all this authority; for it has been given over to me, and I give it to anyone I please. If you, then, will worship me, it will all be yours.' Jesus answered him, 'It is written,

"Worship the Lord your God,
    and serve only him."'

Then the devil took him to Jerusalem, and placed him on the pinnacle of the temple, saying to him, 'If you are the Son of God, throw yourself down from here, for it is written,

"He will command his angels concerning you,
    to protect you",

and

"On their hands they will bear you up,
>   so that you will not dash your foot against
>   a stone."'

Jesus answered him, 'It is said, "Do not put the Lord your God to the test."' When the devil had finished every test, he departed from him until an opportune time.

- After his baptism, Jesus, filled with the Holy Spirit, is led into a place of solitude for his final preparation for his mission. We read that Jesus invited his apostles to come apart into a quiet place, which was to be with himself. It is helpful for us regularly to go aside from the busyness of life into a quiet place for reflection and prayer.

- Temptation is always a question of self-identity. We are defined by what we do rather than what we say. As followers of Christ we try to live by a certain moral code but there are certain things we still fail to do. Let us pray for the grace to seek and to do always the will of God for us.

Monday 10 March
Matthew 25:31–46

Jesus said to them, 'When the Son of Man comes in his glory, and all the angels with him, then he will sit on the throne of his glory. All the nations will be gathered before him, and he will separate people one from another as a shepherd separates the sheep from the goats, and he will put the sheep at his right hand and the goats at the left. Then the king will say to those at his right hand, "Come, you that are blessed by my Father, inherit the kingdom prepared for you from the foundation of the world; for I was hungry and you gave me food, I was thirsty and you gave me something to drink, I was a stranger and you welcomed me, I was naked and you gave me clothing, I was sick and you took care of me, I was in prison and you visited me." Then the righteous will answer him, "Lord, when was it that we saw you hungry and gave you food, or thirsty and gave you something to drink? And when was it that we saw you a stranger and welcomed you, or naked and gave you clothing? And when was it that we saw you sick or in prison and visited you?" And the king will answer them, "Truly I tell you, just as you did it to one of the least of these who are members of my family, you did it to me." Then he will say to those at his left hand, "You that are accursed, depart from me into the eternal fire prepared for the devil and his angels; for I was hungry and you gave me no food, I was thirsty and you gave me nothing to drink, I was a stranger and you did not welcome me, naked and you did not give me clothing, sick and in prison and you did not visit me." Then they also will answer, "Lord, when was it that we saw you hungry or thirsty or a stranger or naked

or sick or in prison, and did not take care of you?"
Then he will answer them, "Truly I tell you, just as
you did not do it to one of the least of these, you did
not do it to me." And these will go away into eternal
punishment, but the righteous into eternal life.'

- Everyone that we meet is always so much more
than what we see with our eyes. They are loved
into life and held in existence by the infinite love
of God for them. St John the Evangelist wrote,
'Those who say, "I love God", and hate their brothers or sisters, are liars; for those who do not love
a brother or sister whom they have seen, cannot
love God whom they have not seen' (1 John 4:20).

Tuesday 11 March
Matthew 6:7–15

Jesus said to them, 'When you are praying, do not
heap up empty phrases as the Gentiles do; for they
think that they will be heard because of their many
words. Do not be like them, for your Father knows
what you need before you ask him.

'Pray then in this way:
  Our Father in heaven,
      hallowed be your name.
      Your kingdom come.
      Your will be done,
          on earth as it is in heaven.

Give us this day our daily bread.
And forgive us our debts,
    as we also have forgiven our debtors.
And do not bring us to the time of trial,
    but rescue us from the evil one.
For if you forgive others their trespasses, your heavenly Father will also forgive you; but if you do not forgive others, neither will your Father forgive your trespasses.'

- Prayer is never a mere recitation of words no matter how much we repeat them. It is a disposition of the heart. In Isaiah we read, 'These people draw near with their mouths and honour me with their lips, while their hearts are far from me.' The most important thing we can do in prayer is to love. This can be done even without words in silent adoration. When we find it difficult to know what to say to the Lord in prayer, let us have him say to us, 'I don't need your words. I just want your company and your love.'

- In the Our Father, Jesus teaches us the right attitude to have in prayer, that God has the first place in our lives, that we have forgiveness in our hearts for others, and that we ask him to provide for and protect us. The First Principle in the Spiritual Exercises of St Ignatius begins 'Man is created to praise, reverence and serve God our Lord, and by this means to save his soul.'

Wednesday 12 March
Luke 11:29–32

When the crowds were increasing, he began to say, 'This generation is an evil generation; it asks for a sign, but no sign will be given to it except the sign of Jonah. For just as Jonah became a sign to the people of Nineveh, so the Son of Man will be to this generation. The queen of the South will rise at the judgement with the people of this generation and condemn them, because she came from the ends of the earth to listen to the wisdom of Solomon, and see, something greater than Solomon is here! The people of Nineveh will rise up at the judgement with this generation and condemn it, because they repented at the proclamation of Jonah, and see, something greater than Jonah is here!'

- Today people will still flock to see external signs and wonders, but the true sign for all Christians will always be the figure of Christ on his cross. 'As Moses lifted up the serpent in the wilderness, so must the Son of Man be lifted up' (John 3:14). 'And I, when I am lifted up from the earth, will draw all people to myself' (John 12:32). And this is how Jesus wants us to remember him. When he said at the Last Supper, 'Do this in remembrance of me', he wanted us to recall his life-giving sacrifice on the cross.

- Truly, 'something greater than Solomon is here'. Every time we come to prayer we are being invited to a private audience with someone greater than anyone else on the planet.

Thursday 13 March
Matthew 7:7–12

Jesus said to them, 'Ask, and it will be given to you; search, and you will find; knock, and the door will be opened for you. For everyone who asks receives, and everyone who searches finds, and for everyone who knocks, the door will be opened. Is there anyone among you who, if your child asks for bread, will give a stone? Or if the child asks for a fish, will give a snake? If you then, who are evil, know how to give good gifts to your children, how much more will your Father in heaven give good things to those who ask him!

'In everything do to others as you would have them do to you; for this is the law and the prophets.'

- It is for the deepest desires in our hearts that we should earnestly ask God in prayer. Ask, search, knock at the door. He will always hear these prayers and answer in the way that is best for us. 'When you search for me, you will find me; if you seek me with all your heart' (Jeremiah 29:13). Like a good parent, our Heavenly Father will provide for us.

- 'In everything do to others as you would have them do to you.' We rightly call this the golden rule, and it reminds us again that our relationship with God is always linked with our relationships with all whom we meet. We are called to live out of our prayer and to pray out of our living.

Friday 14 March
Matthew 5:20–26

Jesus said to them, 'For I tell you, unless your righteousness exceeds that of the scribes and Pharisees, you will never enter the kingdom of heaven.

'You have heard that it was said to those of ancient times, "You shall not murder"; and "whoever murders shall be liable to judgement." But I say to you that if you are angry with a brother or sister, you will be liable to judgement; and if you insult a brother or sister, you will be liable to the council; and if you say, "You fool", you will be liable to the hell of fire. So when you are offering your gift at the altar, if you remember that your brother or sister has something against you, leave your gift there before the altar and go; first be reconciled to your brother or sister, and then come and offer your gift. Come to terms quickly with your accuser while you are on the way to court with him, or your accuser may hand you over to the judge, and the judge to the guard, and you will be thrown into prison. Truly I tell you, you will never get out until you have paid the last penny.'

- Jesus came not to abolish the law but to perfect it. Jesus speaks with a new authority that comes from knowing that the Father had sent him. In the new creation of the kingdom of God the standards of right behaviour are indeed set high. 'Be perfect, therefore, as your heavenly Father is perfect.'

- Jesus came to bring peace and reconciliation to all people. If we do not forgive others we will not be forgiven ourselves. When we come to worship with others we should be at peace with them and reconciled in our hearts with those who have injured us. How aware am I that we go to worship God as a people, and that we are saved as a people?

Saturday 15 March
Matthew 5:43–48

Jesus said, 'You have heard that it was said, "You shall love your neighbour and hate your enemy." But I say to you, Love your enemies and pray for those who persecute you, so that you may be children of your Father in heaven; for he makes his sun rise on the evil and on the good, and sends rain on the righteous and on the unrighteous. For if you love those who love you, what reward do you have? Do not even the tax-collectors do the same? And if you greet only your brothers and sisters, what more are you doing than others? Do not even the Gentiles do the same? Be perfect, therefore, as your heavenly Father is perfect.'

- Human beings are very slow to take things in, and we are still growing in our understanding of revelation. God never stops loving all who exist and we are called to be like our heavenly Father. We pray for the grace to see others more and more as God sees them.

- A story from the East tells us of how a tree leaves its scent even upon the axe that is cutting it down. It is not easy to forgive those who have seriously hurt us, but we have the example of Jesus Christ and the many martyrs. On the cross, Jesus prayed for his executioners, 'Father, forgive them; for they do not know what they are doing.' Let us pray for the grace to forgive others and to recognise our own need for forgiveness.

Second Week of Lent
16–22 March 2025

Something to think and pray about each day this week:

Many legends, stories and traditions have grown up over the centuries regarding Ireland's most famous saint. It is necessary, therefore, to separate the man from the myth by returning to St Patrick's own writings, including what has become known as his *Confession*.

In a simple written account, Patrick's trust in God and his gratitude towards him who had achieved so much through such a weak instrument, shine out. This in no way detracts from the unique light his *Confession* casts on this humble missionary of Christ who brought his Gospel of love to the Irish people. A great missionary looked back on his life and saw the labyrinthine pattern of God's wonderful design.

As he reviews his life journey, which he admits was full of faults and shortcomings, and in the apparently haphazard events of his life, so inexplicable when they occurred, he now sees the hand of God at work in which his hidden plan for the salvation of the Irish is realised. No extraordinary wonders marked his progress throughout Ireland, nevertheless, he touched the hearts of young people who flocked to him and committed their lives to following Christ in the priesthood and religious life.

The essential knowledge about a saint lies not so much in dates and places, but rather in his holiness, his values, what inspired him and his spiritual wrestlings. On these points we are well informed. Patrick sets the record straight regarding his mission and underscores the role God had in it. Often misunderstood in the past, Patrick hoped that his readers would finally grasp how he regarded his long, arduous but ultimately successful mission. His story is one of God's grace that leads to wonder and thanksgiving.

Maurice Hogan SSC,
in the preface to Aidan J. Larkin,
The Spiritual Journey of Saint Patrick

The Presence of God

Dear Jesus, I come to you today longing for your presence. I desire to love you as you love me. May nothing ever separate me from you.

Freedom

Lord, grant me the grace to have freedom of the spirit. Cleanse my heart and soul so that I may live joyously in your love.

Consciousness

Where am I with God? With others? Do I have something to be grateful for? Then I give thanks. Is there something I am sorry for? Then I ask forgiveness.

The Word

The word of God comes down to us through the Scriptures. May the Holy Spirit enlighten my mind and my heart to respond to the Gospel teachings. *(Please turn to the Scripture on the following pages. Inspiration points are there, should you need them. When you are ready, return here to continue.)*

Conversation

How has God's word moved me? Has it left me cold? Has it consoled me or moved me to act in a new way? I imagine Jesus standing or sitting beside me; I turn and share my feelings with him.

Conclusion

I thank God for these moments we have spent together and for any insights I have been given concerning the text.

Sunday 16 March
Second Sunday of Lent

Luke 9:28–36

Now about eight days after these sayings Jesus took with him Peter and John and James, and went up on the mountain to pray. And while he was praying, the appearance of his face changed, and his clothes became dazzling white. Suddenly they saw two men, Moses and Elijah, talking to him. They appeared in glory and were speaking of his departure, which he was about to accomplish at Jerusalem. Now Peter and his companions were weighed down with sleep; but since they had stayed awake, they saw his glory and the two men who stood with him. Just as they were leaving him, Peter said to Jesus, 'Master, it is good for us to be here; let us make three dwellings, one for you, one for Moses, and one for Elijah'—not knowing what he said. While he was saying this, a cloud came and overshadowed them; and they were terrified as they entered the cloud. Then from the cloud came a voice that said, 'This is my Son, my Chosen; listen to him!' When the voice had spoken, Jesus was found alone. And they kept silent and in those days told no one any of the things they had seen.

- St Luke tells us about Jesus at prayer more than any of the other evangelists. Here, these three apostles are given this extraordinary experience of Jesus transfigured to strengthen them in the face of his coming suffering and death. Years later St Peter recalls in a letter this experience on the mountain. It highlights for us how the divinity of Jesus was hidden in his humanity. We pray for a deeper understanding of the Incarnation.

- In our praying it is always the risen Lord we encounter and we can truly say, 'Master, it is good for us to be here.' Let us have the Father say to us, 'This is my Son, my Chosen; listen to him!' And let us pray like Samuel, 'Speak, Lord, for your servant is listening.'

Monday 17 March
St Patrick, Patron of Ireland
Luke 5:1–11

Once while Jesus was standing beside the lake of Gennesaret, and the crowd was pressing in on him to hear the word of God, he saw two boats there at the shore of the lake; the fishermen had gone out of them and were washing their nets. He got into one of the boats, the one belonging to Simon, and asked him to put out a little way from the shore. Then he sat down and taught the crowds from the boat. When he had finished speaking, he said to Simon, 'Put out into the deep water and let down your nets for a catch.' Simon answered, 'Master, we have worked all night long but have caught nothing. Yet if you say so, I will let down the nets.' When they had done this, they caught so many fish that their nets were beginning to break. So they signalled to their partners in the other boat to come and help them. And they came and filled both boats, so that they began to sink. But when Simon Peter saw it, he fell down at Jesus' knees, saying, 'Go away from me, Lord, for I am a sinful man!' For he and all who were with him were amazed at the catch of fish that they had taken; and so also were James and John, sons of Zebedee, who were partners with Simon. Then Jesus said to Simon, 'Do not be afraid; from now on you will be catching people.' When they had brought their boats to shore, they left everything and followed him.

- St Patrick's call from God to leave his home and kin and go on his mission to Ireland came out of his early experiences as a slave, minding sheep and learning to pray and to depend on God alone. In his *Confession*, what stand out are his faith and his gratitude to God. It is through our own life experiences that God calls us to follow him in faith and in gratitude.

- At Christ's bidding Peter let out the nets. Pope St John Paul II used this same image in his call for a renewal in the church. In whatever mission our God gives to us we will always succeed if we remain attached to Christ, the true vine. Let us pray for the grace of a deeper trust in his help.

Tuesday 18 March
Matthew 23:1–12

Then Jesus said to the crowds and to his disciples, 'The scribes and the Pharisees sit on Moses' seat; therefore, do whatever they teach you and follow it; but do not do as they do, for they do not practise what they teach. They tie up heavy burdens, hard to bear, and lay them on the shoulders of others; but they themselves are unwilling to lift a finger to move them. They do all their deeds to be seen by others; for they make their phylacteries broad and their fringes long. They love to have the place of honour at banquets and the best seats in the synagogues, and to be greeted with respect in the market-places, and to have people call them rabbi. But you are not to be called rabbi, for you have one teacher, and you are all students. And call no one your father on earth, for you have one Father—the one in heaven. Nor are you to be called instructors, for you have one instructor, the Messiah. The greatest among you will be your servant. All who exalt themselves will be humbled, and all who humble themselves will be exalted.'

- We are all called to preach by how we live our faith. The Pharisees showed their own warped attitudes to the God who had revealed himself to their ancestors. In our own pride and lack of understanding we too often seek to make God in our own image and likeness. Let our constant prayer be, 'Lord, let me see again.'

- Humankind has so often been plagued by false prophets. Here Jesus reminds us that we have only one true teacher, Christ himself, who came, as he told Pilate, to witness to the truth. Let us always keep his words and his life before us in the witness of our own lives to the truth of the message of the Gospels. He alone is the way, the truth and the life.

Wednesday 19 March
St Joseph, Husband of the BVM
Matthew 1:18–21, 24

Now the birth of Jesus the Messiah took place in this way. When his mother Mary had been engaged to Joseph, but before they lived together, she was found to be with child from the Holy Spirit. Her husband Joseph, being a righteous man and unwilling to expose her to public disgrace, planned to dismiss her quietly. But just when he had resolved to do this, an angel of the Lord appeared to him in a dream and said, 'Joseph, son of David, do not be afraid to take Mary as your wife, for the child conceived in her is from the Holy Spirit. She will bear a son, and you are to name him Jesus, for he will save his people from their sins.' . . . When Joseph awoke from sleep, he did as the angel of the Lord commanded him; he took her as his wife.

- It can often happen that people who are living good and upright lives can find themselves in difficult circumstances. Joseph here faces a dilemma. In his genuine caring for Mary he did not want her to be shamed in the village, even though it appeared that she had been unfaithful to him. But God never forsakes us. If we continue to trust him he will show us a way out of our difficulties. Let us look back at various crises in our lives and see the hand of God in their resolution, and give him thanks.

Thursday 20 March
Luke 16:19–31

Jesus said to his disciples, 'There was a rich man who was dressed in purple and fine linen and who feasted sumptuously every day. And at his gate lay a poor man named Lazarus, covered with sores, who longed to satisfy his hunger with what fell from the rich man's table; even the dogs would come and lick his sores. The poor man died and was carried away by the angels to be with Abraham. The rich man also died and was buried. In Hades, where he was being tormented, he looked up and saw Abraham far away with Lazarus by his side. He called out, "Father Abraham, have mercy on me, and send Lazarus to dip the tip of his finger in water and cool my tongue; for I am in agony in these flames." But Abraham said, "Child, remember that during your lifetime you received your good things, and Lazarus in like manner evil things; but now he is comforted here, and you are in agony. Besides all this, between you and us a great chasm has been fixed, so that those who might want to pass from here to you cannot do so, and no one can cross from there to us." He said, "Then, father, I beg you to send him to my father's house—for I have five brothers—that he may warn them, so that they will not also come into this place of torment." Abraham replied, "They have Moses and the prophets; they should listen to them." He said, "No, father Abraham; but if someone goes to them from the dead, they will repent." He said to him, "'If they do not listen to Moses and the prophets, neither will they be convinced even if someone rises from the dead.'"

- In this story of rich man, poor man, there is a civility and even kindliness between the rich man and Abraham, whom he calls his father Abraham, and who in turn calls him his child, but still the consequences of the rich man's selfishness and lack of charity remain in place. God respects our free choices and we have to take responsibility for them. In 2 Corinthians 6 St Paul reminds us, 'Now is the acceptable time.' We pray to use our time on earth well and to live our lives guided by the teaching and example of Jesus Christ who is much greater than Moses and the prophets.

- The rich man is concerned for his brothers but they, like all of us, will face judgement on their lives. He wants someone to come from the next world to warn them. We have in Jesus one who did come back from the dead and who lives with us through his Spirit, but so many do not believe this.

Friday 21 March
Matthew 21:33–43, 45–46

Jesus said to them, 'Listen to another parable. There was a landowner who planted a vineyard, put a fence around it, dug a wine press in it, and built a watch-tower. Then he leased it to tenants and went to another country. When the harvest time had come, he sent his slaves to the tenants to collect his produce. But the tenants seized his slaves and beat one, killed another, and stoned another. Again he sent other slaves, more than the first; and they treated them in the same way. Finally he sent his son to them, saying, "They will respect my son." But when the tenants saw the son, they said to themselves, "This is the heir; come, let us kill him and get his inheritance." So they seized him, threw him out of the vineyard, and killed him. Now when the owner of the vineyard comes, what will he do to those tenants?' They said to him, 'He will put those wretches to a miserable death, and lease the vineyard to other tenants who will give him the produce at the harvest time.'

Jesus said to them, 'Have you never read in the scriptures:

"The stone that the builders rejected
        has become the cornerstone;
this was the Lord's doing,
        and it is amazing in our eyes"?

Therefore I tell you, the kingdom of God will be taken away from you and given to a people that produces the fruits of the kingdom.'

When the chief priests and the Pharisees heard his parables, they realised that he was speaking about them. They wanted to arrest him, but they feared the crowds, because they regarded him as a prophet.

• Even the Pharisees, despite their blindness, could see that this parable was about them, but instead of repenting, their only desire is to get rid of the one who was reminding them of their sins. We are all tenants of this earth, which is God's vineyard, and we are tasked with producing the fruits of the kingdom of God by living truly Christian lives, always aided by God's grace. How well do we use our gifts for the good of others and for the good of our earthly environment?

• In this parable we can see Jesus foretelling his own death and the opening up of the kingdom of God to the gentile world. Again and again Jesus faces the hatred of the Jewish religious leaders and seeks to melt their hard hearts. Are there ways that we allow attachments and stubbornness to block the message of Christ from getting through to us and healing our selfishness?

Saturday 22 March
Luke 15:1–3, 11–32

Now all the tax-collectors and sinners were coming near to listen to him. And the Pharisees and the scribes were grumbling and saying, 'This fellow welcomes sinners and eats with them.'

So he told them this parable: . . .

'There was a man who had two sons. The younger of them said to his father, "Father, give me the share of the property that will belong to me." So he divided his property between them. A few days later the younger son gathered all he had and travelled to a distant country, and there he squandered his property in dissolute living. When he had spent everything, a severe famine took place throughout that country, and he began to be in need. So he went and hired himself out to one of the citizens of that country, who sent him to his fields to feed the pigs. He would gladly have filled himself with the pods that the pigs were eating; and no one gave him anything. But when he came to himself he said, "How many of my father's hired hands have bread enough and to spare, but here I am dying of hunger! I will get up and go to my father, and I will say to him, 'Father, I have sinned against heaven and before you; I am no longer worthy to be called your son; treat me like one of your hired hands.'" So he set off and went to his father. But while he was still far off, his father saw him and was filled with compassion; he ran and put his arms around him and kissed him. Then the son said to him, "Father, I have sinned against heaven and before you; I am no longer worthy to be called your son." But the father said to his slaves, "Quickly, bring out a robe—the best one—and put it on him; put a ring on his finger and sandals on his feet. And get the fatted calf and kill it, and let us eat and celebrate; for this son of mine was dead and is alive again; he was lost and is found!" And they began to celebrate.

'Now his elder son was in the field; and when he came and approached the house, he heard music and dancing. He called one of the slaves and asked what was going on. He replied, "Your brother has come, and your father has killed the fatted calf, because he has got him back safe and sound." Then he became angry and refused to go in. His father came out and began to plead with him. But he answered his father, "Listen! For all these years I have been working like a slave for you, and I have never disobeyed your command; yet you have never given me even a young goat so that I might celebrate with my friends. But when this son of yours came back, who has devoured your property with prostitutes, you killed the fatted calf for him!" Then the father said to him, "Son, you are always with me, and all that is mine is yours. But we had to celebrate and rejoice, because this brother of yours was dead and has come to life; he was lost and has been found."'

• Our God is a God of mercy. The famous painting by Rembrandt of the prodigal son kneeling at the feet of his father, whose hand is gently laid upon him, speaks volumes of the loving and forgiving nature of our heavenly Father. When Pope Francis declared a year of mercy he sought to emphasise this aspect of God. The prophet Hosea wrote, 'What I want is mercy, not sacrifice.' Recognising our own sinfulness, let us place all our trust in the loving mercy of our Father.

- Despite all his years of living with his father, the elder brother did not really know him. His attitude was a legal one of being obedient to the rules and commands of his father but his heart was not with his father. He had only to ask and he could have had a party for himself and his friends at any time, because his father wanted to give him everything. How well do we know this infinitely loving and generous Father who longs to give himself entirely to each of us? St Ignatius advises us 'to ponder with deep affection, how the Lord wishes to give himself to us'.

23–29 March 2025

Something to think and pray about each day this week:

The Annunciation brings us back to the source of Lent: the announcement of the Incarnation and Mary saying 'yes' to her part in it. The mystery that comes to a close in Lent now begins.

The Incarnation is full of people: Mary, Joseph and Elizabeth and the two unborn babies, in the wombs of their mothers, as we all began. God's son would not come on earth without human origins. He had a mother like all of us. We are remembering our beginnings.

Maybe Lent can be about people rather than rituals. We can give time to enjoying family life, putting the emphasis on giving to family and community rather than on wondering what we can get. Lent can be a time to share with those who are needy, a time to meet some of the needs of the wider world. During Lent we can volunteer our time and personal gifts to others. Lent can be a time to listen, to God's word and to one another.

Donal Neary SJ,
The Sacred Heart Messenger,
April 2023

The Presence of God

As I sit here, the beating of my heart, the ebb and flow of my breathing, the movements of my mind are all signs of God's ongoing creation of me. I pause for a moment and become aware of this presence of God within me.

Freedom

I will ask God's help to be free from my own preoccupations, to be open to God in this time of prayer, to come to know, love and serve God more.

Consciousness

At this moment, Lord, I turn my thoughts to you. I will leave aside my chores and preoccupations. I will take rest and refreshment in your presence.

The Word

Now I turn to the Scripture set out for me this day. I read slowly over the words and see if any sentence or sentiment appeals to me. *(Please turn to the Scripture on the following pages. Inspiration points are there, should you need them. When you are ready, return here to continue.)*

Conversation

Begin to talk to Jesus about the Scripture you have just read. What part of it strikes a chord in you? Perhaps the words of a friend—or some story you have heard recently—will slowly rise to the surface of your consciousness. If so, does the story throw light on what the Scripture passage may be saying to you?

Conclusion
Glory be to the Father, and to the Son, and to the Holy Spirit,
As it was in the beginning, is now and ever shall be,
World without end. Amen.

Sunday 23 March
Third Sunday of Lent

Luke 13:1–9

At that very time there were some present who told him about the Galileans whose blood Pilate had mingled with their sacrifices. He asked them, 'Do you think that because these Galileans suffered in this way they were worse sinners than all other Galileans? No, I tell you; but unless you repent, you will all perish as they did. Or those eighteen who were killed when the tower of Siloam fell on them—do you think that they were worse offenders than all the others living in Jerusalem? No, I tell you; but unless you repent, you will all perish just as they did.'

Then he told this parable: 'A man had a fig tree planted in his vineyard; and he came looking for fruit on it and found none. So he said to the gardener, "See here! For three years I have come looking for fruit on this fig tree, and still I find none. Cut it down! Why should it be wasting the soil?" He replied, "Sir, let it alone for one more year, until I dig round it and put manure on it. If it bears fruit next year, well and good; but if not, you can cut it down."'

• During Lent we are invited to reflect on the really important things in life. Our allotted life span is always an unknown. Only God sees the bigger picture of our lives. Our time on earth is indeed a time of grace to prepare for an eternity of happiness, but this time is made up of a series of nows, of moments, none of which will ever come again. 'Carpe diem!—Seize the day!' In the Gospels we are frequently called to watch and pray! Let us do so now.

- The sudden death of friends and the experience of life-threatening illnesses and accidents are all reminders that our sojourn on earth is temporary. Both Jesus and his Father are continually at work in our lives. Let us make good use of the opportunities that are being given to us.

Monday 24 March
Luke 4:24–30

And he said, 'Truly I tell you, no prophet is accepted in the prophet's home town. But the truth is, there were many widows in Israel in the time of Elijah, when the heaven was shut up for three years and six months, and there was a severe famine over all the land; yet Elijah was sent to none of them except to a widow at Zarephath in Sidon. There were also many lepers in Israel in the time of the prophet Elisha, and none of them was cleansed except Naaman the Syrian.' When they heard this, all in the synagogue were filled with rage. They got up, drove him out of the town, and led him to the brow of the hill on which their town was built, so that they might hurl him off the cliff. But he passed through the midst of them and went on his way.

- Is it pride or blindness that blocks us from accepting the truth from other human beings? It has been said, 'There are none so blind as those who will not see.' In this Gospel we also see great anger and resentment in the Nazarenes against the one who had grown up among them, and they try to destroy him. We too are human beings. What are the dark parts in our own hearts?

- Jesus lived a fully human life, with all its ups and downs, joys and sorrows. Let us be with Jesus as he is driven out of his home village by the townspeople, and talk to him about his feelings and great disappointment.

Tuesday 25 March
The Annunciation of the Lord
Luke 1:26–38

In the sixth month the angel Gabriel was sent by God to a town in Galilee called Nazareth, to a virgin engaged to a man whose name was Joseph, of the house of David. The virgin's name was Mary. And he came to her and said, 'Greetings, favoured one! The Lord is with you.' But she was much perplexed by his words and pondered what sort of greeting this might be. The angel said to her, 'Do not be afraid, Mary, for you have found favour with God. And now, you will conceive in your womb and bear a son, and you will name him Jesus. He will be great, and will be called the Son of the Most High, and the Lord God will give to him the throne of his ancestor David. He will reign over the house of Jacob for ever, and of his kingdom there will be no end.' Mary said to the angel, 'How can this be, since I am a virgin?' The angel said to her, 'The Holy Spirit will come upon you, and the power of the Most High will overshadow you; therefore the child to be born will be holy; he will be called Son of God. And now, your relative Elizabeth in her old age has also conceived a son; and this is the sixth month for her who was said to be barren. For nothing will be impossible with God.' Then Mary said, 'Here am I, the servant of the Lord; let it be with me according to your word.' Then the angel departed from her.

• Mary did not understand all that was being asked of her, and Luke tells us she pondered over many things as they unfolded around her. Her 'yes' to God's message was a blanket acceptance in faith of whatever would come in her life. Our own faith and trust in God has to be like that. We will never in this life come to understand the reason for all that happens to us. Our 'yes' to God is a commitment of mind and heart to God. Let us pray to renew our own commitment and to live it.

Wednesday 26 March
Matthew 5:17–19

Jesus said to his disciples, 'Do not think that I have come to abolish the law or the prophets; I have come not to abolish but to fulfil. For truly I tell you, until heaven and earth pass away, not one letter, not one stroke of a letter, will pass from the law until all is accomplished. Therefore, whoever breaks one of the least of these commandments, and teaches others to do the same, will be called least in the kingdom of heaven; but whoever does them and teaches them will be called great in the kingdom of heaven.'

- God's revelation about himself and what he was asking of us came only gradually over a very long period. The keeping of the law and the prophets could never be enough to redeem and save us. Christ alone could do this, but by living according to the law and prophets the people of God were being prepared for the later acceptance of the teaching of Jesus, who came with a new and unique authority to complete and to fulfil the law. It is Christ that we now look to in our seeking to live what God is asking of us.

- Lord Jesus, help us to live according to your teachings and your example and to practise what we profess in our faith.

Thursday 27 March
Luke 11:14–23

Now he was casting out a demon that was mute; when the demon had gone out, the one who had been mute spoke, and the crowds were amazed. But some of them said, 'He casts out demons by Beelzebul, the ruler of the demons.' Others, to test him, kept demanding from him a sign from heaven. But he knew what they were thinking and said to them, 'Every kingdom divided against itself becomes a desert, and house falls on house. If Satan also is divided against himself, how will his kingdom stand?—for you say that I cast out the demons by Beelzebul. Now if I cast out the demons by Beelzebul, by whom do your exorcists cast them out? Therefore they will be your judges. But if it is by the finger of God that I cast out the demons, then the kingdom of God has come to you. When a strong man, fully armed, guards his castle, his property is safe. But when one stronger than he attacks him and overpowers him, he takes away his armour in which he trusted and divides his plunder. Whoever is not with me is against me, and whoever does not gather with me scatters.'

- The sheer logic of Christ's argument should have been enough to make his opponents reflect on their position. However, for their own selfish reasons they did not want to be with him. Let us pray to grasp more deeply our own littleness and lack of understanding.

- In the Gospels Jesus cast out many evil spirits. Pope Francis has agreed that we can change the translation at the end of the Our Father, so I now find it more helpful to say, 'And lead us in time of temptation and deliver us from the evil one.' The image of our God leading us by the hand can be very helpful in our prayer. It is mentioned in Psalms 63 and 73, and in Mark 8:23, when Jesus leads the blind man by the hand out of the village at Bethsaida.

Friday 28 March
Mark 12:28–34

One of the scribes came near and heard them disputing with one another, and seeing that he answered them well, he asked him, 'Which commandment is the first of all?' Jesus answered, 'The first is, "Hear, O Israel: the Lord our God, the Lord is one; you shall love the Lord your God with all your heart, and with all your soul, and with all your mind, and with all your strength." The second is this, "You shall love your neighbour as yourself." There is no other commandment greater than these.' Then the scribe said to him, 'You are right, Teacher; you have truly said that "he is one, and besides him there is no other"; and "to love him with all the heart, and with all the understanding, and with all the strength", and "to love one's neighbour as oneself",—this is much more important than all whole burnt-offerings and sacrifices.' When Jesus saw that he answered wisely, he said to him, 'You are not far from the kingdom of God.' After that no one dared to ask him any question.

- It is very rare in the Gospels to find our Lord praising one of the scribes. It can be said that our Lord reduced all the commandments to two, namely love God and love your neighbour. They are really two parts of the one great commandment to love, as it is out of a loving heart that we love both God and neighbour. In the order of things God must always come first. Do I always put God in the first place in my life? He can never take second place.

Saturday 29 March
Luke 18:9–14

He also told this parable to some who trusted in themselves that they were righteous and regarded others with contempt: 'Two men went up to the temple to pray, one a Pharisee and the other a tax-collector. The Pharisee, standing by himself, was praying thus, "God,

I thank you that I am not like other people: thieves, rogues, adulterers, or even like this tax-collector. I fast twice a week; I give a tenth of all my income." But the tax-collector, standing far off, would not even look up to heaven, but was beating his breast and saying, "God, be merciful to me, a sinner!" I tell you, this man went down to his home justified rather than the other; for all who exalt themselves will be humbled, but all who humble themselves will be exalted.'

- Here Jesus gives a very important lesson about prayer. For our prayers to be heard we must always pray with humility before our God. Humility is truth, the truth of our own littleness and complete dependence on God. It is in this attitude that we come now before God to pray from our hearts.

- In his prayer the Pharisee focused on himself and all he had done. The tax collector focused on God and his great mercy. St Teresa of Ávila taught that real prayer is more about loving than thinking. There is a lot of truth in the statement that when we are thinking in prayer we are with ourselves, and when we are loving in prayer we are with God. Prayer is all about a relationship. Do I go to prayer just to ask for things for myself and others, or do I spend most of my time staying with the Lord, sharing with him and listening to him?

Fourth Week of Lent
30 March–5 April 2025

Something to think and pray about each day this week:

'What are you giving up for Lent?' 'Sweets!' Childish? Of course. As a child, though, to go forty days without sweets was a serious commitment.

There is so much more to Lent. The child in us may give up sweets, but the faithful part of us is called to a place of reflection and repentance, where we take stock and accept what we find, a storeroom from which is brought out the old and the new, where we might find memories of more faith-filled and innocent days, when going to church and blessing our face came naturally.

As well as 'giving up' for Lent is there a place for 'taking up' too? Taking up a more positive outlook, taking up again the call to Sunday Mass? Is there room on the Lenten journey for a bit of social justice, outreach, charity, volunteerism? Space to make a difference in the lives of others? Maybe, if we can forgive a little, love a lot, share more, pray sincerely, be involved, we will find that instead of giving up sweets, a spiritual sweetness, a true sense of wellness, will envelop us.

Vincent Sherlock,
The Sacred Heart Messenger,
February 2023

The Presence of God

'Be still, and know that I am God!' Lord, your words lead us to the calmness and greatness of your presence.

Freedom

God is not foreign to my freedom. The Spirit breathes life into my most intimate desires, gently nudging me towards all that is good. I ask for the grace to let myself be enfolded by the Spirit.

Consciousness

Where do I sense hope, encouragement and growth in my life? By looking back over the past few months, I may be able to see which activities and occasions have produced rich fruit. If I do notice such areas, I will determine to give those areas both time and space in the future.

The Word

The word of God comes down to us through the Scriptures. May the Holy Spirit enlighten my mind and my heart to respond to the Gospel teachings. *(Please turn to the Scripture on the following pages. Inspiration points are there, should you need them. When you are ready, return here to continue.)*

Conversation
What is stirring in me as I pray? Am I consoled, troubled, left cold? I imagine Jesus standing or sitting at my side, and I share my feelings with him.

Conclusion
Glory be to the Father, and to the Son, and to the Holy Spirit,
As it was in the beginning, is now and ever shall be,
World without end. Amen.

Sunday 30 March
Fourth Sunday of Lent

Luke 15:1–3, 11–32

Now all the tax-collectors and sinners were coming near to listen to him. And the Pharisees and the scribes were grumbling and saying, 'This fellow welcomes sinners and eats with them.'

So he told them this parable: . . . 'There was a man who had two sons. The younger of them said to his father, "Father, give me the share of the property that will belong to me." So he divided his property between them. A few days later the younger son gathered all he had and travelled to a distant country, and there he squandered his property in dissolute living. When he had spent everything, a severe famine took place throughout that country, and he began to be in need. So he went and hired himself out to one of the citizens of that country, who sent him to his fields to feed the pigs. He would gladly have filled himself with the pods that the pigs were eating; and no one gave him anything. But when he came to himself he said, "How many of my father's hired hands have bread enough and to spare, but here I am dying of hunger! I will get up and go to my father, and I will say to him, 'Father, I have sinned against heaven and before you; I am no longer worthy to be called your son; treat me like one of your hired hands.'" So he set off and went to his father. But while he was still far off, his father saw him and was filled with compassion; he ran and put his arms around him and kissed him. Then the son said to him, "Father, I have sinned against heaven and before you; I am no longer worthy to be called your son." But the father said to his slaves, "Quickly, bring out a robe—the best one—and put it on him; put a ring on his finger and sandals on his feet. And get the fatted calf and kill it, and let us eat and celebrate; for this son of mine was dead and is alive again; he was lost and is found!" And they began to celebrate.

'Now his elder son was in the field; and when he came and approached the house, he heard music and dancing. He called one of the slaves and asked what was going on. He replied, "Your brother has come, and your father has killed the fatted calf, because he has got him back safe and sound." Then he became angry and refused to go in. His father came out and began to plead with him. But he answered his father, "Listen! For all these years I have been working like a slave for you, and I have never disobeyed your command; yet you have never given me even a young goat so that I might celebrate with my friends. But when this son of yours came back, who has devoured your property with prostitutes, you killed the fatted calf for him!" Then the father said to him, "Son, you are always with me, and all that is mine is yours. But we had to celebrate and rejoice, because this brother of yours was dead and has come to life; he was lost and has been found."'

- The marginalised and sinners found something very attractive in Jesus and they came in droves to listen to him. They sensed his love and compassion for them. This beautiful story of the father and his wayward son epitomises these qualities in Jesus. Jesus came to reveal the Father to us. Our God is a God of infinite love and compassion. In this season of Lent, when we reflect on our own waywardness, let us kneel at his feet and acknowledge our need for his mercy and help.

- The elder brother, while keeping all the rules, had closed his heart to the call to be compassionate and forgiving. Are there attitudes in my life that block me from hearing this same call to me?

Monday 31 March
John 4:43–54

When the two days were over, he went from that place to Galilee (for Jesus himself had testified that a prophet has no honour in the prophet's own country). When he came to Galilee, the Galileans welcomed him, since they had seen all that he had done in Jerusalem at the festival; for they too had gone to the festival.

Then he came again to Cana in Galilee where he had changed the water into wine. Now there was a royal official whose son lay ill in Capernaum. When he heard that Jesus had come from Judea to Galilee, he went and begged him to come down and heal his son, for he was at the point of death. Then Jesus said to him, 'Unless you see signs and wonders you will not believe.' The official said to him, 'Sir, come down before my little boy dies.' Jesus said to him, 'Go; your son will live.' The man believed the word that Jesus spoke to him and started on his way. As he was going down, his slaves met him and told him that his child was alive. So he asked them the hour when he began to recover, and they said to him, 'Yesterday at one in the afternoon the fever left him.' The father realised that this was the hour when Jesus had said to him, 'Your son will live.' So he himself believed, along with his whole household. Now this was the second sign that Jesus did after coming from Judea to Galilee.

• St John's Gospel has been called the book of signs—this is the second sign Jesus gave of his divinity. The royal official immediately took Jesus at his word and believed that his son would be cured. Too often we are like 'doubting Thomas', who said he would not believe unless he could see the mark of the nails and could touch the risen Jesus. Let us pray to be among those who are blessed because although they have not seen, yet they believe.

Tuesday 1 April
John 5:1–3, 5–16

After this there was a festival of the Jews, and Jesus went up to Jerusalem.

Now in Jerusalem by the Sheep Gate there is a pool, called in Hebrew Beth-zatha, which has five porticoes. In these lay many invalids—blind, lame, and paralysed. . . . One man was there who had been ill for thirty-eight years. When Jesus saw him lying there and knew that he had been there a long time, he said to him, 'Do you want to be made well?' The sick man answered him, 'Sir, I have no one to put me into the pool when the water is stirred up; and while I am making my way, someone else steps down ahead of me.' Jesus said to him, 'Stand up, take your mat and walk.' At once the man was made well, and he took up his mat and began to walk.

Now that day was a sabbath. So the Jews said to the man who had been cured, 'It is the sabbath; it is not lawful for you to carry your mat.' But he answered them, 'The man who made me well said to me, "Take up your mat and walk."' They asked him, 'Who is the man who said to you, "Take it up and walk"?' Now the man who had been healed did not know who it was, for Jesus had disappeared in the crowd that was there. Later Jesus found him in the temple and said to him, 'See, you have been made well! Do not sin any more, so that nothing worse happens to you.' The man went away and told the Jews that it was Jesus who had made him well. Therefore the Jews started persecuting Jesus, because he was doing such things on the sabbath.

- The fact that Jesus asked the invalid if he wanted to be cured showed great sensitivity. An invalid for almost forty years, he would face many big changes in his life if suddenly made well again. We should be careful with what we ask for in prayer. The request of Jesus in the garden of Gethsemane was followed each time with, 'Yet, not my will but yours be done.' Let us ask God to give us whatever he knows is best for us.

- The Jewish religious leaders made many laws that they claimed were to honour God but in reality were to give themselves authority and control over people's lives. Jesus, knowing their hypocrisy, ignored these laws. Our human laws should always be motivated by love and compassion for the welfare of all. In my dealings with others do I put human laws above the good of others? Do I season justice with mercy?

Wednesday 2 April
John 5:17–30

But Jesus answered them, 'My Father is still working, and I also am working.' For this reason the Jews were seeking all the more to kill him, because he was not only breaking the sabbath, but was also calling God his own Father, thereby making himself equal to God.

Jesus said to them, 'Very truly, I tell you, the Son can do nothing on his own, but only what he sees the Father doing; for whatever the Father does, the Son does likewise. The Father loves the Son and shows him all that he himself is doing; and he will show him greater works than these, so that you will be astonished. Indeed, just as the Father raises the dead and gives them life, so also the Son gives life to whomsoever he wishes. The Father judges no one but has given all judgement to the Son, so that all may honour the Son just as they honour the Father. Anyone who does not honour the Son does not honour the Father who sent him. Very truly, I tell you, anyone who hears my word and believes him who sent me has eternal life, and does not come under judgement, but has passed from death to life.

'Very truly, I tell you, the hour is coming, and is now here, when the dead will hear the voice of the Son of God, and those who hear will live. For just as the Father has life in himself, so he has granted the Son also to have life in himself; and he has given him authority to execute judgement, because he is the Son of Man. Do not be astonished at this; for the hour is coming when all who are in their graves will hear his voice and will come out—those who have done good, to the resurrection of life, and those who have done evil, to the resurrection of condemnation.

'I can do nothing on my own. As I hear, I judge; and my judgement is just, because I seek to do not my own will but the will of him who sent me.'

- St John's Gospel, written after the other three Gospels, is unequalled in making clear the divinity of Jesus and his close relationship with his Father in heaven. At the end of chapter 20 he states that this Gospel was written that we may come to believe that Jesus is the Messiah and the Son of God. Jesus told us he sought always to do the will of his Father. As followers of Jesus this should always be our aim.

- Without God holding us in existence every moment of our lives, we simply would cease to exist. This working in us is the work of the whole Trinity, Father, Son and Holy Spirit. As we read in Luke 12:7, every hair on our heads is counted. Let us pray to have complete trust in the unchanging love of God for every one of us.

Thursday 3 April
John 5:31–47

Jesus said to them, 'If I testify about myself, my testimony is not true. There is another who testifies on my behalf, and I know that his testimony to me is true. You sent messengers to John, and he testified to the truth. Not that I accept such human testimony, but I say these things so that you may be saved. He was a burning and shining lamp, and you were willing to rejoice for a while in his light. But I have a testimony greater than John's. The works that the Father has given me to complete, the very works that I am doing, testify on my behalf that the Father has sent me. And the Father who sent me has himself testified on my behalf. You have never heard his voice or seen his form, and you do not have his word abiding in you, because you do not believe him whom he has sent.

'You search the scriptures because you think that in them you have eternal life; and it is they that testify on my behalf. Yet you refuse to come to me to have life. I do not accept glory from human beings. But I know that you do not have the love of God in you. I have come in my Father's name, and you do not accept me; if another comes in his own name, you will accept him. How can you believe when you accept glory from one another and do not seek the glory that comes from the one who alone is God? Do not think that I will accuse you before the Father; your accuser is Moses, on whom you have set your hope. If you believed Moses, you would believe me, for he wrote about me. But if you do not believe what he wrote, how will you believe what I say?'

- What we do defines who and what we are more than any words we may use. Jesus told Pilate that he had come to witness to the truth. He did this not only through what he preached but even more by what he did. 'The very works that I am doing, testify on my behalf.' Jesus told us that his disciples are those who do the will of his Father, not those who call out, 'Lord, Lord.' We ask God to help us to be true to the name of his Son and to ourselves by how we live.

• In his love for his enemies Jesus tried hard to save them but they deliberately closed their ears and hearts to him. To reject Jesus Christ is to reject the One who sent him. Here Jesus tells them, 'I know that you do not have the love of God in you.' Let us pray for a greater love of God.

Friday 4 April
John 7:1–2, 10, 25–30

After this Jesus went about in Galilee. He did not wish to go about in Judea because the Jews were looking for an opportunity to kill him. Now the Jewish festival of Booths was near. . . .

But after his brothers had gone to the festival, then he also went, not publicly but as it were in secret. . . .

Now some of the people of Jerusalem were saying, 'Is not this the man whom they are trying to kill? And here he is, speaking openly, but they say nothing to him! Can it be that the authorities really know that this is the Messiah? Yet we know where this man is from; but when the Messiah comes, no one will know where he is from.' Then Jesus cried out as he was teaching in the temple, 'You know me, and you know where I am from. I have not come on my own. But the one who sent me is true, and you do not know him. I know him, because I am from him, and he sent me.' Then they tried to arrest him, but no one laid hands on him, because his hour had not yet come.

- Jesus, knowing the bloodthirsty nature of his opponents, walked a tightrope. He knew he was destined to suffer and be killed but that would only be in the fullness of time. For now he would continue to carry out his mission from his Father, which was to spread the Good News of the kingdom at whatever cost to himself. In the end he paid a heavy price. Are we willing to take up our cross each day and witness to our faith, despite ridicule and even persecution?

Saturday 5 April
John 7:40–52

When they heard these words, some in the crowd said, 'This is really the prophet.' Others said, 'This is the Messiah.' But some asked, 'Surely the Messiah does not come from Galilee, does he? Has not the scripture said that the Messiah is descended from David and comes from Bethlehem, the village where David lived?' So there was a division in the crowd because of him. Some of them wanted to arrest him, but no one laid hands on him.

Then the temple police went back to the chief priests and Pharisees, who asked them, 'Why did you not arrest him?' The police answered, 'Never has anyone spoken like this!' Then the Pharisees replied, 'Surely you have not been deceived too, have you? Has any one of the authorities or of the Pharisees believed in him? But this crowd, which does not know the law—they are accursed.' Nicodemus, who had gone to Jesus before, and who was one of them, asked, 'Our law does not judge people without first giving them a hearing to find out what they are doing, does it?' They replied, 'Surely you are not also from Galilee, are you? Search and you will see that no prophet is to arise from Galilee.'

- A closed mind is a great affliction, all the more so when it is reinforced by pride. These so-called 'learned men' were so convinced of their own rightness in interpreting the Scriptures, nothing that Jesus said or did could get through to them. St John Henry Newman said, 'To live is to change, and to live well is to change often.' How willing am I to let go of the addictions and selfishness that block God's working in me?

- Even the police, sent to arrest him, acknowledged that 'Never has anyone spoken like this!' Let us open ourselves to the teachings of Jesus and say to him, 'Speak, Lord, for your servant is listening.'

Fifth Week of Lent
6–12 April 2025

Something to think and pray about each day this week:

Lent is a time to respond to that hunger which lies at the core of our being, the hunger for a deeper connection with the Creator, the hunger to experience freshness in our lives, the hunger for what we truly long for. What better place to work all of this out than 'the wilderness'? From time to time, we are landed in the wilderness. Sometimes it is an unpleasant experience and at other times we crave it, in response to a deep desire to step back from the day-to-day and make space in our lives for reflection.

Tríona Doherty and Jane Mellett,
The Deep End: A Journey with the Sunday Gospels
in the Year of Mark

The Presence of God

'Come to me, all you that are weary and are carrying heavy burdens, and I will give you rest.' Here I am, Lord. I come to seek your presence. I long for your healing power.

Freedom

By God's grace I was born to live in freedom. Free to enjoy the pleasures he created for me. Dear Lord, grant that I may live as you intended, with complete confidence in your loving care.

Consciousness

Knowing that God loves me unconditionally, I look honestly over the past day, its events, and my feelings. Do I have something to be grateful for? Then I give thanks. Is there something I am sorry for? Then I ask forgiveness.

The Word

God speaks to each of us individually. I listen attentively to hear what he is saying to me. Read the text a few times, then listen. *(Please turn to the Scripture on the following pages. Inspiration points are there, should you need them. When you are ready, return here to continue.)*

Conversation
I know with certainty that there were times when you carried me, Lord. There were times when it was through your strength that I got through the dark times in my life.

Conclusion
Glory be to the Father, and to the Son, and to the Holy Spirit,
As it was in the beginning, is now and ever shall be,
World without end. Amen.

Sunday 6 April
Fifth Sunday of Lent

John 8:1–11

Then each of them went home, while Jesus went to the Mount of Olives. Early in the morning he came again to the temple. All the people came to him and he sat down and began to teach them. The scribes and the Pharisees brought a woman who had been caught in adultery; and making her stand before all of them, they said to him, 'Teacher, this woman was caught in the very act of committing adultery. Now in the law Moses commanded us to stone such women. Now what do you say?' They said this to test him, so that they might have some charge to bring against him. Jesus bent down and wrote with his finger on the ground. When they kept on questioning him, he straightened up and said to them, 'Let anyone among you who is without sin be the first to throw a stone at her.' And once again he bent down and wrote on the ground. When they heard it, they went away, one by one, beginning with the elders; and Jesus was left alone with the woman standing before him. Jesus straightened up and said to her, 'Woman, where are they? Has no one condemned you?' She said, 'No one, sir.' And Jesus said, 'Neither do I condemn you. Go your way, and from now on do not sin again.'

- During this last week of his life, when his hearers went home to their houses, Jesus spent his nights at the foot of the Mount of Olives in the garden of Gethsemane, praying and sleeping. Early each morning he set out for the temple for his day's work of preaching and teaching, at daily risk of arrest. In our meeting with him now in prayer we can dialogue with him about what this last week was like.

- Jesus always loved the sinner and not the sin. 'Neither do I condemn you. Go your way, and from now on do not sin again.' The Gospel of John says elsewhere that God did not send the Son to condemn the world but to save it. Let us pray to imitate him in his great mercy.

Monday 7 April

John 8:12–20

Again Jesus spoke to them, saying, 'I am the light of the world. Whoever follows me will never walk in darkness but will have the light of life.' Then the Pharisees said to him, 'You are testifying on your own behalf; your testimony is not valid.' Jesus answered, 'Even if I testify on my own behalf, my testimony is valid because I know where I have come from and where I am going, but you do not know where I come from or where I am going. You judge by human standards; I judge no one. Yet even if I do judge, my judgement is valid; for it is not I alone who judge, but I and the Father who sent me. In your law it is written that the testimony of two witnesses is valid. I testify on my own behalf, and the Father who sent me testifies on my behalf.' Then they said to him, 'Where is your Father?' Jesus answered, 'You know neither me nor my Father. If you knew me, you would know my Father also.' He spoke these words while he was teaching in the treasury of the temple, but no one arrested him, because his hour had not yet come.

- 'You know neither me nor my Father.' We cannot love someone we do not know. Our God wants us to come to know him, and knowing him will inevitably lead us to love him who is infinitely loveable. 'For I desire steadfast love and not sacrifice, the knowledge of God rather than burnt-offerings.' (Hosea 6:6). Let us pray to be open to our God revealing himself to us as Jesus promised that he would in John 14:21.

Tuesday 8 April
John 8:21–30

Again he said to them, 'I am going away, and you will search for me, but you will die in your sin. Where I am going, you cannot come.' Then the Jews said, 'Is he going to kill himself? Is that what he means by saying, "Where I am going, you cannot come"?' He said to them, 'You are from below, I am from above; you are of this world, I am not of this world. I told you that you would die in your sins, for you will die in your sins unless you believe that I am he.' They said to him, 'Who are you?' Jesus said to them, 'Why do I speak to you at all? I have much to say about you and much to condemn; but the one who sent me is true, and I declare to the world what I have heard from him.' They did not understand that he was speaking to them about the Father. So Jesus said, 'When you have lifted up the Son of Man, then you will realise that I am he, and that I do nothing on my own, but I speak these things as the Father instructed me. And the one who sent me is with me; he has not left me alone, for I always do what is pleasing to him.' As he was saying these things, many believed in him.

- At his trial Jesus told Pilate that his kingdom was not of this world. Here Jesus speaks of how he has come from his Father and speaks what his Father wants him to speak. Jesus is the fullness of God's revelation to us. Let us pray to learn how to listen to him and to place him always at the centre of our lives.

Wednesday 9 April

John 8:31–42

Then Jesus said to the Jews who had believed in him, 'If you continue in my word, you are truly my disciples; and you will know the truth, and the truth will make you free.' They answered him, 'We are descendants of Abraham and have never been slaves to anyone. What do you mean by saying, "You will be made free"?'

Jesus answered them, 'Very truly, I tell you, everyone who commits sin is a slave to sin. The slave does not have a permanent place in the household; the son has a place there for ever. So if the Son makes you free, you will be free indeed. I know that you are descendants of Abraham; yet you look for an opportunity to kill me, because there is no place in you for my word. I declare what I have seen in the Father's presence; as for you, you should do what you have heard from the Father.'

They answered him, 'Abraham is our father.' Jesus said to them, 'If you were Abraham's children, you would be doing what Abraham did, but now you are trying to kill me, a man who has told you the truth that I heard from God. This is not what Abraham did. You are indeed doing what your father does.' They said to him, 'We are not illegitimate children; we have one father, God himself.' Jesus said to them, 'If God were your Father, you would love me, for I came from God and now I am here. I did not come on my own, but he sent me.'

- In their blindness and pride the Jews could not see their own wrongdoing and lack of compassion.

Despite the witness of his deeds they refused to accept the words of Jesus when he told them he had been sent by the Father. Our faith is a commitment we make to God without having all the answers to our many questions. We grow in this faith by using it and, especially, by spending time in real prayer from our hearts. 'We believe; help our unbelief.'

Thursday 10 April

John 8:51–59

Jesus said to them, 'Very truly, I tell you, whoever keeps my word will never see death.' The Jews said to him, 'Now we know that you have a demon. Abraham died, and so did the prophets; yet you say, "Whoever keeps my word will never taste death." Are you greater than our father Abraham, who died? The prophets also died. Who do you claim to be?' Jesus answered, 'If I glorify myself, my glory is nothing. It is my Father who glorifies me, he of whom you say, "He is our God", though you do not know him. But I know him; if I were to say that I do not know him, I would be a liar like you. But I do know him and I keep his word. Your ancestor Abraham rejoiced that he would see my day; he saw it and was glad.' Then the Jews said to him, 'You are not yet fifty years old, and have you seen Abraham?' Jesus said to them,

'Very truly, I tell you, before Abraham was, I am.' So they picked up stones to throw at him, but Jesus hid himself and went out of the temple.

- Yet again, in this Gospel we see the two levels at work. When Jesus speaks of life he is speaking about the life of the soul that goes on for eternity. But for the Jews it is the earthly life of the body that is uppermost in their minds, hence the references to Abraham being dead and the age of Jesus. We have to put on the mind of Christ and give priority to the life of the soul. Let us speak to the Lord about this, asking for a greater understanding.

Friday 11 April
John 10:31–42

The Jews took up stones again to stone him. Jesus replied, 'I have shown you many good works from the Father. For which of these are you going to stone me?' The Jews answered, 'It is not for a good work that we are going to stone you, but for blasphemy, because you, though only a human being, are making yourself God.' Jesus answered, 'Is it not written in your law, "I said, you are gods"? If those to whom the word of God came were called "gods"—and the scripture cannot be annulled—can you say that the one whom the Father has sanctified and sent into the world is blaspheming because I said, "I am God's Son"? If I am not doing the works of my Father, then do not believe me. But if I do them, even though you do not believe me, believe the works, so that you may know and understand that the Father is in me and I am in the Father.' Then they tried to arrest him again, but he escaped from their hands.

He went away again across the Jordan to the place where John had been baptizing earlier, and he remained there. Many came to him, and they were saying, 'John performed no sign, but everything that John said about this man was true.' And many believed in him there.

• Jesus appeals to his hearers to judge the truth of his words by the witness of his doing the good works of his Father. 'You will know them by their fruits.' This is too much for the scribes and Pharisees in their hardness of heart. 'Unless you change and become like children you will never enter the kingdom of heaven.' Let us pray for the gift of humility and to recognise the truth of our own littleness.

Saturday 12 April
John 11:45–56

Many of the Jews therefore, who had come with Mary and had seen what Jesus did, believed in him. But some of them went to the Pharisees and told them what he had done. So the chief priests and the Pharisees called a meeting of the council, and said, 'What are we to do? This man is performing many signs. If we let him go on like this, everyone will believe in him, and the Romans will come and destroy both our holy place and our nation.' But one of them, Caiaphas, who was high priest that year, said to them, 'You know nothing at all! You do not understand that it is better for you to have one man die for the people than to have the whole nation destroyed.' He did not say this on his own, but being high priest that year he prophesied that Jesus was about to die for the nation, and not for the nation only, but to gather into one the dispersed children of God. So from that day on they planned to put him to death.

Jesus therefore no longer walked about openly among the Jews, but went from there to a town called Ephraim in the region near the wilderness; and he remained there with the disciples.

Now the Passover of the Jews was near, and many went up from the country to Jerusalem before the Passover to purify themselves. They were looking for Jesus and were asking one another as they stood in the temple, 'What do you think? Surely he will not come to the festival, will he?'

- The members of the Sanhedrin were aware of the signs Jesus was performing but they failed to see where they were pointing to. Let us pray to be able to read the signs of our times, and to see our need for God.

- The Jewish religious leaders could find only one solution to the problem of Jesus and that was to kill him. Even though it failed for them, many human beings have continued down the centuries to apply this same solution to rid themselves of problems. That there is a darkness in the heart of humankind is undoubted. Let us pray that the light of Christ and the illumination of the Holy Spirit will transform the hearts of all.

Holy Week
13–19 April 2025

Something to think and pray about each day this week:

There are two bowls of water in the story of the Passion. One is Pilate's, used to scrub himself of all responsibility. The other is the one with which Jesus bathes others, soaking them in lavish love.

The two bowls are always before us in life. Jesus shows us that when you take the side of the dispossessed, your spirit deepens and grows. To pick up the towel is not to become a doormat. We are called, not to serve people's wants, but their needs. We serve others in the name of Christ. We share what we have, but, more importantly, who we are, especially with people who are rejected and alienated. They are the life presence that transforms us by showing us the heart of God, the prophets, preachers and provocative witnesses of the Gospel. They challenge us with questions that disturb and disquiet, and we see the Passion and Easter with new eyes and hearts.

Easter invites us to remember the Lord when we gather as a community for the Eucharist. He entrusts his future in the world to us in the Church.

John Cullen,
The Sacred Heart Messenger,
April 2022

The Presence of God

'Be still, and know that I am God!' Lord, your words lead us to the calmness and greatness of your presence.

Freedom

Leave me here freely all alone. / In cell where never sunlight shone. / Should no one ever speak to me. / This golden silence makes me free!

> —Part of a poem by Bl Titus Brandsma, written while he was a prisoner at Dachau concentration camp

Consciousness

Knowing that God loves me unconditionally, I can afford to be honest about how I am. How has the day been, and how do I feel now? I share my feelings openly with the Lord.

The Word

I take my time to read the word of God slowly, a few times, allowing myself to dwell on anything that strikes me. *(Please turn to the Scripture on the following pages. Inspiration points are there, should you need them. When you are ready, return here to continue.)*

Conversation
Sometimes I wonder what I might say if I were to meet you in person, Lord. I think I might say, 'Thank you', because you are always there for me.

Conclusion
I thank God for these moments we have spent together and for any insights I have been given concerning the text.

Sunday 13 April
Palm Sunday of the Passion of the Lord
Luke 22:14—23:56

When the hour came, he took his place at the table, and the apostles with him. He said to them, 'I have eagerly desired to eat this Passover with you before I suffer; for I tell you, I will not eat it until it is fulfilled in the kingdom of God.' Then he took a cup, and after giving thanks he said, 'Take this and divide it among yourselves; for I tell you that from now on I will not drink of the fruit of the vine until the kingdom of God comes.' Then he took a loaf of bread, and when he had given thanks, he broke it and gave it to them, saying, 'This is my body, which is given for you. Do this in remembrance of me.' And he did the same with the cup after supper, saying, 'This cup that is poured out for you is the new covenant in my blood. But see, the one who betrays me is with me, and his hand is on the table. For the Son of Man is going as it has been determined, but woe to that one by whom he is betrayed!' Then they began to ask one another which one of them it could be who would do this.

A dispute also arose among them as to which one of them was to be regarded as the greatest. But he said to them, 'The kings of the Gentiles lord it over them; and those in authority over them are called benefactors. But not so with you; rather the greatest among you must become like the youngest, and the leader like one who serves. For who is greater, the one who is at the table or the one who serves? Is it not the one at the table? But I am among you as one who serves.

'You are those who have stood by me in my trials; and I confer on you, just as my Father has conferred on me, a kingdom, so that you may eat and drink at my table in my kingdom, and you will sit on thrones judging the twelve tribes of Israel.

'Simon, Simon, listen! Satan has demanded to sift all of you like wheat, but I have prayed for you that your own faith may not fail; and you, when once you have turned back, strengthen your brothers.' And he said to him, 'Lord, I am ready to go with you to prison and to death!' Jesus said, 'I tell you, Peter, the cock will not crow this day, until you have denied three times that you know me.'

He said to them, 'When I sent you out without a purse, bag, or sandals, did you lack anything?' They said, 'No, not a thing.' He said to them, 'But now, the one who has a purse must take it, and likewise a bag. And the one who has no sword must sell his cloak and buy one. For I tell you, this scripture must be fulfilled in me, "And he was counted among the lawless"; and indeed what is written about me is being fulfilled.' They said, 'Lord, look, here are two swords.' He replied, 'It is enough.'

He came out and went, as was his custom, to the Mount of Olives; and the disciples followed him. When he reached the place, he said to them, 'Pray that you may not come into the time of trial.' Then he withdrew from them about a stone's throw, knelt down, and prayed, 'Father, if you are willing, remove this cup from me; yet, not my will but yours be done.' [Then an angel from heaven appeared to him and gave him strength. In his anguish he prayed more earnestly, and his sweat became like great drops of blood falling down on the ground.] When he got up from prayer, he came to the disciples and found them sleeping because of grief, and he said to them, 'Why are you sleeping? Get up and pray that you may not come into the time of trial.'

While he was still speaking, suddenly a crowd came, and the one called Judas, one of the twelve, was leading them. He approached Jesus to kiss him; but Jesus said to him, 'Judas, is it with a kiss that you are betraying the Son of Man?' When those who were around him saw what was coming, they asked, 'Lord, should we strike with the sword?' Then one of them struck the slave of the high priest and cut off his right ear. But Jesus said, 'No more of this!' And he touched his ear and healed him. Then Jesus said to the chief priests, the officers of the temple police, and the elders who had come for him, 'Have you come out with swords and clubs as if I were a bandit? When I was with you day after day in the temple, you did not lay hands on me. But this is your hour, and the power of darkness!'

Then they seized him and led him away, bringing him into the high priest's house. But Peter was following at a distance. When they had kindled a fire in the middle of the courtyard and sat down together, Peter sat among them. Then a servant-girl, seeing him in the firelight, stared at him and said, 'This man also was with him.' But he denied it, saying, 'Woman, I do not know him.' A little later someone else, on seeing him, said, 'You also are one of them.' But Peter said, 'Man, I am not!' Then about an hour later yet another kept insisting, 'Surely this man also was with him; for he is a Galilean.' But Peter said, 'Man, I do not know what you are talking about!' At that moment, while he was still speaking, the cock crowed. The Lord turned and looked at Peter. Then Peter remembered the word of the Lord, how he had said to him, 'Before the cock crows today, you will deny me three times.' And he went out and wept bitterly.

Now the men who were holding Jesus began to mock him and beat him; they also blindfolded him and kept asking him, 'Prophesy! Who is it that struck you?' They kept heaping many other insults on him.

When day came, the assembly of the elders of the people, both chief priests and scribes, gathered together, and they brought him to their council. They said, 'If you are the Messiah, tell us.' He replied, 'If I tell you, you will not believe; and if I question you, you will not answer. But from now on the Son of Man will be seated at the right hand of the power of God.' All of them asked, 'Are you, then, the Son of God?' He said to them, 'You say that I am.' Then they said, 'What further testimony do we need? We have heard it ourselves from his own lips!'

Then the assembly rose as a body and brought Jesus before Pilate. They began to accuse him, saying, 'We found this man perverting our nation, forbidding us to pay taxes to the emperor, and saying that he himself is the Messiah, a king.' Then Pilate asked him, 'Are you the king of the Jews?' He answered, 'You say so.' Then Pilate said to the chief priests and the crowds, 'I find no basis for an accusation against this man.' But they were insistent and said, 'He stirs up the people by teaching throughout all Judea, from Galilee where he began even to this place.'

When Pilate heard this, he asked whether the man was a Galilean. And when he learned that he was under Herod's jurisdiction, he sent him off to Herod, who was himself in Jerusalem at that time. When Herod saw Jesus, he was very glad, for he had been wanting to see him for a long time, because he had heard about him and was hoping to see him perform some sign. He questioned him at some length, but Jesus gave him no answer. The chief priests and the scribes stood by, vehemently accusing him. Even Herod with his soldiers treated him with contempt and mocked him; then he put an elegant robe on him, and sent him back to Pilate. That same day Herod and Pilate became friends with each other; before this they had been enemies.

Pilate then called together the chief priests, the leaders, and the people, and said to them, 'You brought me this man as one who was perverting the people; and here I have examined him in your presence and have not found this man guilty of any of your charges against him. Neither has Herod, for he sent him back to us. Indeed, he has done nothing to deserve death. I will therefore have him flogged and release him.'

Then they all shouted out together, 'Away with this fellow! Release Barabbas for us!' (This was a man who had been put in prison for an insurrection that had taken place in the city, and for murder.) Pilate, wanting to release Jesus, addressed them again; but they kept shouting, 'Crucify, crucify him!' A third time he said to them, 'Why, what evil has he done? I have found in him no ground for the sentence of death; I will therefore have him flogged and then release him.' But they kept urgently demanding with loud shouts that he should be crucified; and their voices prevailed.

So Pilate gave his verdict that their demand should be granted. He released the man they asked for, the one who had been put in prison for insurrection and murder, and he handed Jesus over as they wished.

As they led him away, they seized a man, Simon of Cyrene, who was coming from the country, and they laid the cross on him, and made him carry it behind Jesus. A great number of the people followed him, and among them were women who were beating their breasts and wailing for him. But Jesus turned to them and said, 'Daughters of Jerusalem, do not weep for me, but weep for yourselves and for your children. For the days are surely coming when they will say, "Blessed are the barren, and the wombs that never bore, and the breasts that never nursed." Then they will begin to say to the mountains, "Fall on us"; and to the hills, "Cover us." For if they do this when the wood is green, what will happen when it is dry?'

Two others also, who were criminals, were led away to be put to death with him. When they came to the place that is called The Skull, they crucified Jesus there with the criminals, one on his right and one on his left. [Then Jesus said, 'Father, forgive them; for they do not know what they are doing.'] And they cast lots to divide his clothing. And the people stood by, watching; but the leaders scoffed at him, saying, 'He saved others; let him save himself if he is the Messiah of God, his chosen one!' The soldiers also mocked him, coming up and offering him sour wine, and saying, 'If you are the King of the Jews, save yourself!' There was also an inscription over him, 'This is the King of the Jews.'

One of the criminals who were hanged there kept deriding him and saying, 'Are you not the Messiah? Save yourself and us!' But the other rebuked him, saying, 'Do you not fear God, since you are under the same sentence of condemnation? And we indeed have been condemned justly, for we are getting what we deserve for our deeds, but this man has done nothing wrong.' Then he said, 'Jesus, remember me when you come into your kingdom.' He replied, 'Truly I tell you, today you will be with me in Paradise.'

It was now about noon, and darkness came over the whole land until three in the afternoon, while the sun's light failed; and the curtain of the temple was torn in two. Then Jesus, crying with a loud voice, said, 'Father, into your hands I commend my spirit.' Having said this, he breathed his last. When the centurion saw what had taken place, he praised God and said, 'Certainly this man was innocent.' And when all the crowds who had gathered there for this spectacle saw what had taken place, they returned home, beating their breasts. But all his acquaintances, including the women who had followed him from Galilee, stood at a distance, watching these things.

Now there was a good and righteous man named Joseph, who, though a member of the council, had not agreed to their plan and action. He came from the Jewish town of Arimathea, and he was waiting expectantly for the kingdom of God. This man went to Pilate and asked for the body of Jesus. Then he took it down, wrapped it in a linen cloth, and laid it in a rock-hewn tomb where no one had ever been laid. It was the day of Preparation, and the sabbath was beginning. The women who had come with him from Galilee followed, and they saw the tomb and how his body was laid. Then they returned, and prepared spices and ointments.

On the sabbath they rested according to the commandment.

- Our praying on the Passion can be a most unselfish prayer as we focus not on our own needs but on the sufferings of our Saviour. For prayer we can take any of the Gospel accounts, or the Stations of the Cross, or the sorrowful mysteries of the Rosary.

- What was it like as a human being to feel the pain of being crucified? 'Father, forgive them; for they do not know what they are doing.' Jesus never stopped loving those who crucified him.

Monday 14 April

John 12:1–11

Six days before the Passover Jesus came to Bethany, the home of Lazarus, whom he had raised from the dead. There they gave a dinner for him. Martha served, and Lazarus was one of those at the table with him. Mary took a pound of costly perfume made of pure nard, anointed Jesus' feet, and wiped them with her hair. The house was filled with the fragrance of the perfume. But Judas Iscariot, one of his disciples (the one who was about to betray him), said, 'Why was this perfume not sold for three hundred denarii and the money given to the poor?' (He said this not because he cared about the poor, but because he was a thief; he kept the common purse and used to steal what was put into it.) Jesus said, 'Leave her alone. She bought it so that she might keep it for the day of my burial. You always have the poor with you, but you do not always have me.'

When the great crowd of the Jews learned that he was there, they came not only because of Jesus but also to see Lazarus, whom he had raised from the dead. So the chief priests planned to put Lazarus to death as well, since it was on account of him that many of the Jews were deserting and were believing in Jesus.

- In the home of Martha and Mary Jesus found a great welcome and a reverence which drew him back to visit them. Let us pray for the grace to make him welcome in our hearts, and to be enabled to make our home in him, as he has invited us to do.

• Despite being called to the inner circle of Jesus' apostles, Judas in his selfishness had not taken his opportunities to come to know and love him. Now is the acceptable time for each of us to come to know and love and follow Jesus our Lord and Master.

Tuesday 15 April
John 13:21–33, 36–38

After saying this Jesus was troubled in spirit, and declared, 'Very truly, I tell you, one of you will betray me.' The disciples looked at one another, uncertain of whom he was speaking. One of his disciples—the one whom Jesus loved—was reclining next to him; Simon Peter therefore motioned to him to ask Jesus of whom he was speaking. So while reclining next to Jesus, he asked him, 'Lord, who is it?' Jesus answered, 'It is the one to whom I give this piece of bread when I have dipped it in the dish.' So when he had dipped the piece of bread, he gave it to Judas son of Simon Iscariot. After he received the piece of bread, Satan entered into him. Jesus said to him, 'Do quickly what you are going to do.' Now no one at the table knew why he said this to him. Some thought that, because

Judas had the common purse, Jesus was telling him, 'Buy what we need for the festival'; or, that he should give something to the poor. So, after receiving the piece of bread, he immediately went out. And it was night.

When he had gone out, Jesus said, 'Now the Son of Man has been glorified, and God has been glorified in him. If God has been glorified in him, God will also glorify him in himself and will glorify him at once. Little children, I am with you only a little longer. You will look for me; and as I said to the Jews so now I say to you, 'Where I am going, you cannot come.' . . .

Simon Peter said to him, 'Lord, where are you going?' Jesus answered, 'Where I am going, you cannot follow me now; but you will follow afterwards.' Peter said to him, 'Lord, why can I not follow you now? I will lay down my life for you.' Jesus answered, 'Will you lay down your life for me? Very truly, I tell you, before the cock crows, you will have denied me three times.'

- To know that one of his own close companions was about to betray him to his enemies must have been a great sadness for Jesus. In Psalm 55:13–15 we read of the treachery of one who had walked in harmony with him in the house of God.

- That Peter too would so soon deny even knowing him, despite saying he would lay down his life for him, would also be a source of sadness for Jesus. So often we, like St Peter, profess our faith and, indeed, our love for Jesus, but fail to live this in our lives. We ask for a deep sorrow for our fickleness and our failure to be true to him.

Wednesday 16 April
Matthew 26:14–25

Then one of the twelve, who was called Judas Iscariot, went to the chief priests and said, 'What will you give me if I betray him to you?' They paid him thirty pieces of silver. And from that moment he began to look for an opportunity to betray him.

On the first day of Unleavened Bread the disciples came to Jesus, saying, 'Where do you want us to make the preparations for you to eat the Passover?' He said, 'Go into the city to a certain man, and say to him, "The Teacher says, My time is near; I will keep the Passover at your house with my disciples."' So the disciples did as Jesus had directed them, and they prepared the Passover meal.

When it was evening, he took his place with the twelve; and while they were eating, he said, 'Truly I tell you, one of you will betray me.' And they became greatly distressed and began to say to him one after another, 'Surely not I, Lord?' He answered, 'The one who has dipped his hand into the bowl with me will betray me. The Son of Man goes as it is written of him, but woe to that one by whom the Son of Man is betrayed! It would have been better for that one not to have been born.' Judas, who betrayed him, said, 'Surely not I, Rabbi?' He replied, 'You have said so.'

• We are told that Judas used to steal from the common purse. Now his greed has increased and he wants even more money. It is frightening, especially for those consecrated to God in religious life or the priesthood, that despite his privileged call Judas could still sin so grievously. St Paul in Philippians 2 tells his converts to 'work out your own salvation with fear and trembling'. We are all sinners, always in need of God's mercy and grace.

Thursday 17 April
Holy Thursday
John 13:1–15

Now before the festival of the Passover, Jesus knew that his hour had come to depart from this world and go to the Father. Having loved his own who were in the world, he loved them to the end. The devil had already put it into the heart of Judas son of Simon Iscariot to betray him. And during supper Jesus, knowing that the Father had given all things into his hands, and that he had come from God and was going to God, got up from the table, took off his outer robe, and tied a towel around himself. Then he poured water into a basin and began to wash the disciples' feet and to wipe them with the towel that was tied around him. He came to Simon Peter, who said to him, 'Lord, are you going to wash my feet?' Jesus answered, 'You do not know now what I am doing, but later you will understand.' Peter said to him, 'You will never wash my feet.' Jesus answered, 'Unless I wash you, you have no share with me.' Simon Peter said to him, 'Lord, not my feet only but also my hands and my head!' Jesus said to him, 'One who has bathed does not need to wash, except for the feet, but is entirely clean. And you are clean, though not all of you.' For he knew who was to betray him; for this reason he said, 'Not all of you are clean.'

After he had washed their feet, had put on his robe, and had returned to the table, he said to them, 'Do you know what I have done to you? You call me Teacher and Lord—and you are right, for that is what I am. So if I, your Lord and Teacher, have washed your feet, you also ought to wash one another's feet. For I have set you an example, that you also should do as I have done to you.'

- Actions speak louder than words. Not only the teaching but also the example of Jesus, our Lord and Master, is always the headline for all his followers. He told us that he came not to be served but to serve and here he shows it. And he said that the greatest among us are those who serve the weakest. Lord, help us to see that whatever kindness and help we show to others you take it as done to you.

Friday 18 April
Good Friday
John 18:1—19:42

After Jesus had spoken these words, he went out with his disciples across the Kidron valley to a place where there was a garden, which he and his disciples entered. Now Judas, who betrayed him, also knew the place, because Jesus often met there with his disciples. So Judas brought a detachment of soldiers together with police from the chief priests and the Pharisees, and they came there with lanterns and torches and weapons. Then Jesus, knowing all that was to happen to him, came forward and asked them, 'For whom are you looking?' They answered, 'Jesus of Nazareth.' Jesus replied, 'I am he.' Judas, who betrayed him, was standing with them. When Jesus said to them, 'I am he', they stepped back and fell to the ground. Again he asked them, 'For whom are you looking?' And they said, 'Jesus of Nazareth.' Jesus answered, 'I told you that I am he. So if you are looking for me, let these men go.' This was to fulfil the word that he had spoken, 'I did not lose a single one of those whom you gave me.' Then Simon Peter, who had a sword, drew it, struck the high priest's slave, and cut off his right ear. The slave's name was Malchus. Jesus said to Peter, 'Put your sword back into its sheath. Am I not to drink the cup that the Father has given me?'

So the soldiers, their officer, and the Jewish police arrested Jesus and bound him. First they took him to Annas, who was the father-in-law of Caiaphas, the high priest that year. Caiaphas was the one who had advised the Jews that it was better to have one person die for the people.

Simon Peter and another disciple followed Jesus. Since that disciple was known to the high priest, he went with Jesus into the courtyard of the high priest, but Peter was standing outside at the gate. So the other disciple, who was known to the high priest, went out, spoke to the woman who guarded the gate, and brought Peter in. The woman said to Peter, 'You are not also one of this man's disciples, are you?' He said, 'I am not.' Now the slaves and the police had made a charcoal fire because it was cold, and they were standing round it and warming themselves. Peter also was standing with them and warming himself.

Then the high priest questioned Jesus about his disciples and about his teaching. Jesus answered, 'I have spoken openly to the world; I have always taught in synagogues and in the temple, where all the Jews come together. I have said nothing in secret. Why do you ask me? Ask those who heard what I said to them; they know what I said.' When he had said this, one of the police standing nearby struck Jesus on the face, saying, 'Is that how you answer the high priest?' Jesus answered, 'If I have spoken wrongly, testify to the wrong. But if I have spoken rightly, why do you strike me?' Then Annas sent him bound to Caiaphas the high priest.

Now Simon Peter was standing and warming himself. They asked him, 'You are not also one of his disciples, are you?' He denied it and said, 'I am not.' One of the slaves of the high priest, a relative of the man whose ear Peter had cut off, asked, 'Did I not see you in the garden with him?' Again Peter denied it, and at that moment the cock crowed.

Then they took Jesus from Caiaphas to Pilate's headquarters. It was early in the morning. They themselves did not enter the headquarters, so as to avoid ritual defilement and to be able to eat the Passover. So Pilate went out to them and said, 'What accusation do you bring against this man?' They answered, 'If this man were not a criminal, we would not have handed him over to you.' Pilate said to them, 'Take him yourselves and judge him according to your law.'

The Jews replied, 'We are not permitted to put any-one to death.' (This was to fulfil what Jesus had said when he indicated the kind of death he was to die.)

Then Pilate entered the headquarters again, summoned Jesus, and asked him, 'Are you the King of the Jews?' Jesus answered, 'Do you ask this on your own, or did others tell you about me?' Pilate replied, 'I am not a Jew, am I? Your own nation and the chief priests have handed you over to me. What have you done?' Jesus answered, 'My kingdom is not from this world. If my kingdom were from this world, my followers would be fighting to keep me from being handed over to the Jews. But as it is, my kingdom is not from here.' Pilate asked him, 'So you are a king?' Jesus answered, 'You say that I am a king. For this I was born, and for this I came into the world, to tes-tify to the truth. Everyone who belongs to the truth listens to my voice.' Pilate asked him, 'What is truth?'

After he had said this, he went out to the Jews again and told them, 'I find no case against him. But you have a custom that I release someone for you at the Passover. Do you want me to release for you the King of the Jews?' They shouted in reply, 'Not this man, but Barabbas!' Now Barabbas was a bandit.

Then Pilate took Jesus and had him flogged. And the soldiers wove a crown of thorns and put it on his head, and they dressed him in a purple robe. They kept coming up to him, saying, 'Hail, King of the

Jews!' and striking him on the face. Pilate went out again and said to them, 'Look, I am bringing him out to you to let you know that I find no case against him.' So Jesus came out, wearing the crown of thorns and the purple robe. Pilate said to them, 'Here is the man!' When the chief priests and the police saw him, they shouted, 'Crucify him! Crucify him!' Pilate said to them, 'Take him yourselves and crucify him; I find no case against him.' The Jews answered him, 'We have a law, and according to that law he ought to die because he has claimed to be the Son of God.'

Now when Pilate heard this, he was more afraid than ever. He entered his headquarters again and asked Jesus, 'Where are you from?' But Jesus gave him no answer. Pilate therefore said to him, 'Do you refuse to speak to me? Do you not know that I have power to release you, and power to crucify you?' Jesus answered him, 'You would have no power over me unless it had been given you from above; therefore the one who handed me over to you is guilty of a greater sin.' From then on Pilate tried to release him, but the Jews cried out, 'If you release this man, you are no friend of the emperor. Everyone who claims to be a king sets himself against the emperor.'

When Pilate heard these words, he brought Jesus outside and sat on the judge's bench at a place called The Stone Pavement, or in Hebrew Gabbatha. Now it was the day of Preparation for the Passover; and it was about noon. He said to the Jews, 'Here is your King!' They cried out, 'Away with him! Away with him! Crucify him!' Pilate asked them, 'Shall I crucify your King?' The chief priests answered, 'We have no king but the emperor.' Then he handed him over to them to be crucified.

So they took Jesus; and carrying the cross by himself, he went out to what is called The Place of the Skull, which in Hebrew is called Golgotha. There they crucified him, and with him two others, one on either side, with Jesus between them. Pilate also had an inscription written and put on the cross. It read, 'Jesus of Nazareth, the King of the Jews.' Many of the Jews read this inscription, because the place where Jesus was crucified was near the city; and it was written in Hebrew, in Latin, and in Greek. Then the chief priests of the Jews said to Pilate, 'Do not write, "The King of the Jews", but, "This man said, I am King of the Jews."' Pilate answered, 'What I have written I have written.' When the soldiers had crucified Jesus, they took his clothes and divided them into four parts, one for each soldier. They also took his tunic; now the tunic was seamless, woven in one piece from the top. So they said to one another, 'Let us not tear it, but cast lots for it to see who will get it.' This was to fulfil what the scripture says,

'They divided my clothes among themselves,
   and for my clothing they cast lots.'
And that is what the soldiers did.

Meanwhile, standing near the cross of Jesus were his mother, and his mother's sister, Mary the wife of Clopas, and Mary Magdalene. When Jesus saw his mother and the disciple whom he loved standing beside her, he said to his mother, 'Woman, here is your son.' Then he said to the disciple, 'Here is your mother.' And from that hour the disciple took her into his own home.

After this, when Jesus knew that all was now finished, he said (in order to fulfil the scripture), 'I am thirsty.' A jar full of sour wine was standing there. So they put a sponge full of the wine on a branch of hyssop and held it to his mouth. When Jesus had received the wine, he said, 'It is finished.' Then he bowed his head and gave up his spirit.

Since it was the day of Preparation, the Jews did not want the bodies left on the cross during the sabbath, especially because that sabbath was a day of great solemnity. So they asked Pilate to have the legs of the crucified men broken and the bodies removed. Then the soldiers came and broke the legs of the first and of the other who had been crucified with him. But when they came to Jesus and saw that he was already dead, they did not break his legs. Instead, one of the soldiers pierced his side with a spear, and at once blood and water came out. (He who saw this has testified so that you also may believe. His testimony is true, and he knows that he tells the truth.)

These things occurred so that the scripture might be fulfilled, 'None of his bones shall be broken.' And again another passage of scripture says, 'They will look on the one whom they have pierced.'

After these things, Joseph of Arimathea, who was a disciple of Jesus, though a secret one because of his fear of the Jews, asked Pilate to let him take away the body of Jesus. Pilate gave him permission; so he came and removed his body. Nicodemus, who had at first come to Jesus by night, also came, bringing a mixture of myrrh and aloes, weighing about a hundred pounds. They took the body of Jesus and wrapped it with the spices in linen cloths, according to the burial custom of the Jews. Now there was a garden in the place where he was crucified, and in the garden there was a new tomb in which no one had ever been laid. And so, because it was the Jewish day of Preparation, and the tomb was nearby, they laid Jesus there.

- The gospel story of the life, death and resurrection of Jesus is truly the story of a life given up for others. At the Last Supper he said, 'This is my body, which is given *for you*,' and, 'This cup that is poured out *for you* is the new covenant in my blood.' Let us consider any part of the Passion now, and ask for a deep compassion with Jesus in his suffering and to accompany him in it.

- Fr Pedro Arrupe SJ, a former father general of the Society of Jesus, wrote that we cannot be fair-weather friends of Jesus. We must be willing to enter with him into the cloud of Calvary and to watch and pray with him.

Saturday 19 April
Holy Saturday
Luke 24:1–12

But on the first day of the week, at early dawn, they came to the tomb, taking the spices that they had prepared. They found the stone rolled away from the tomb, but when they went in, they did not find the body. While they were perplexed about this, suddenly two men in dazzling clothes stood beside them. The women were terrified and bowed their faces to the ground, but the men said to them, 'Why do you look for the living among the dead? He is not here, but has risen. Remember how he told you, while he was still in Galilee, that the Son of Man must be handed over to sinners, and be crucified, and on the third day rise again.' Then they remembered his words, and return-ing from the tomb, they told all this to the eleven and to all the rest. Now it was Mary Magdalene, Joanna, Mary the mother of James, and the other women with them who told this to the apostles. But these words seemed to them an idle tale, and they did not believe them. But Peter got up and ran to the tomb; stooping and looking in, he saw the linen cloths by themselves; then he went home, amazed at what had happened.

- The first Holy Saturday must have been a day of stunned silence for the mother of Jesus and for his disciples. In the Jewish understanding, a person's end was an indication of how they had lived. In the Book of Wisdom 2:16–17 we read, 'He . . . boasts that God is his father . . . let us test what will happen at the end of his life.' Let us spend some time now in prayer with Mary and the apostles, sharing in the mood of sombreness and waiting for the dawn of Easter Sunday.

Sunday 20 April
Easter Sunday of the Resurrection of the Lord
John 20:1–9

Early on the first day of the week, while it was still dark, Mary Magdalene came to the tomb and saw that the stone had been removed from the tomb. So she ran and went to Simon Peter and the other disciple, the one whom Jesus loved, and said to them, 'They have taken the Lord out of the tomb, and we do not know where they have laid him.' Then Peter and the other disciple set out and went towards the tomb. The two were running together, but the other disciple outran Peter and reached the tomb first. He bent down to look in and saw the linen wrappings lying there, but he did not go in. Then Simon Peter came, following him, and went into the tomb. He saw the linen wrappings lying there, and the cloth that had been on Jesus' head, not lying with the linen wrappings but rolled up in a place by itself. Then the other disciple, who reached the tomb first, also went in, and he saw and believed; for as yet they did not understand the scripture, that he must rise from the dead.

- 'Enough! The Resurrection. A heart's-clarion! Away grief's gasping, joyless days, dejection. Across my foundering deck shone a beacon, an eternal beam.' So wrote the poet Gerard Manley Hopkins SJ about the comfort of the Resurrection. The darkness of sin and death is forever shattered by the 'eternal beam' of Easter morning. We open our hearts to the joy of Christ's victory, and we give immense thanks to God.

- Jesus had foretold his rising from the dead and now everything has changed. He is vindicated in his triumph over those who opposed him. We all share in the victory of Jesus, our Brother, and all the graces that we could ever need have been won for us. Like the apostles who ran to the tomb, let us allow the enormity of this event to seep into our souls as we now meet our Saviour in prayer.

Suscipe

Take, Lord, and receive all my liberty,
my memory, my understanding,
and my entire will,
all I have and call my own.

You have given all to me.
To you, Lord, I return it.

Everything is yours; do with it what you will.
Give me only your love and your grace;
that is enough for me.

—St. Ignatius of Loyola

Prayer to Know God's Will

May it please the supreme and divine Goodness
To give us all abundant grace
Ever to know his most holy will
And perfectly to fulfill it.

—St. Ignatius of Loyola